Ultimate ear TRAINING

FOR GUITAR & BASS

BY GARY WILLIS

T0051157

To access audio visit:
www.halleonard.com/mylibrary

3702-7643-0663-8945

ISBN 978-0-7935-8156-6

HAL•LEONARD®

Visit Hal Leonard Online at
www.halleonard.com

Contact us:
Hal Leonard
7777 West Bluemound Road
Milwaukee, WI 53213
Email: info@halleonard.com

In Europe, contact:
Hal Leonard Europe Limited
42 Wigmore Street
Marylebone, London, W1U 2RN
Email: info@halleonardeurope.com

In Australia, contact:
Hal Leonard Australia Pty. Ltd.
4 Lentara Court
Cheltenham, Victoria, 3192 Australia
Email: info@halleonard.com.au

Table of Contents

Introduction

Over the years, many aspiring musicians have asked me what is the most important aspect of music to work on. Usually, they expect me to say "groove," "technique," "reading," "theory," etc. While these are all important chops to have together, I think the most valuable asset that a musician can have is a well-developed ear. If you were a painter, your most important sense would be your vision. You would need well-trained eyes in order to recognize things like color, composition, shapes, balance, etc. Once you were able to recognize these things at work in other paintings, you'd be much better equipped to put them together and make them work for you. So it is with music, too.

One thing we all have in common is that music communicates to us through our ears. However, in order for *you* to communicate using music, you need to be able to translate what you imagine *into your hands*. That means connecting your ear to your instrument. In this book, the connection process is broken down into three parts:

1) Manufacturing

This is the core of ear training. "Manufacturing drills" will develop your ability to internally create and know the the sound without your instrument. Throughout much of this book, I'll be asking you to put your instrument down. You shouldn't let yourself become too dependent on the bass or guitar to know if you're hearing things correctly; after all, you don't want to have to stop the band every time you get an idea and then "hunt and peck" until you get it right. Although the connection we want to establish is the one between your ears and your instrument, before that happens, you need to make sure your ears are giving you reliable information. That's where your voice comes in.

My voice? Don't worry, you don't have to develop an outstanding singing voice in order to have a good ear; I'm a great example of that. My singing career (background vocals) lasted one rehearsal. The vocal line went up, and the bass line went down. I was a one-man train wreck and was kindly thanked to not sing anymore. Think of your own voice as a kind of measuring stick for notes. You only need it to be accurate enough that you can imitate and evaluate what you hear. Once that skill is developed, you'll have a self-contained way of understanding what you hear that's independent of your instrument.

2) Visualization

This is the second step in the process—where we begin to connect our ears to our instruments and make ear training truly practical. You see, as we learn how to identify and sing intervals, scales, and chords, we'll also learn to imagine, or *visualize,* how they appear on the fretboard. Bassists will concentrate on single-octave scale patterns. Guitarists will use two patterns—the bass pattern and an upper octave unique to the guitar. "Visualization tests" will then assess your ability to "see" what you're hearing on the instrument.

3) Imitation

"Imitation exercises" are the last step; they'll ask you to put it all together. You'll internalize the sound, visualize the sound, then play it on your instrument.

The value of this whole process comes from developing your ear to such an extent that when you hear something you'll be able to play it. At that point, whatever you *imagine* you'll be able to *play* as well.

The Major Scale
Intervals and Labels

Intervals are the distances between notes. When you listen to music, you're listening to intervals. They happen between the notes of a chord, simultaneously, and between the notes of a melody line, sequentially. The system for labeling intervals is a part of music history that's been around for over 300 years. It may not be the most logical, but it's the one everybody uses, so we've got to learn to work with it.

The first group of intervals and labels that we'll work with comes from the *major scale*. You've probably heard the major scale before, but just in case, here's what one sounds like:

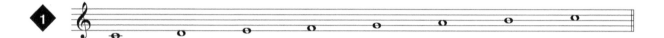

The first note in the scale that you heard is the *root*. The label for most of the intervals from the root to the other notes in the scale use the word major.

Here are the intervals created from the root:

 1. From the root to the second note in the scale is called a *major 2nd*.

2. From the root to the third note in the scale is called a *major 3rd*.

3. From the root to the fourth note in the scale is called a *perfect 4th*.

4. From the root to the fifth note in the scale is called a *perfect 5th*.

5. From the root to the sixth note in the scale is called a *major 6th*.

6. From the root to the seventh note in the scale is called a *major 7th*.

7. From the root to the eighth note in the scale is called a *perfect octave*.

Notice that the only intervals above that are not major are called "perfect." Here's where the labeling system starts to show its age. Since the Catholic church was in charge of pretty much all music 300 years ago, the 4th, 5th, and octave were deemed "holy" and acceptable (a.k.a. "perfect") intervals, unlike some of the other chromatic "heathen" intervals we'll study later.

By the way, the interval from a note to the same note is called a *perfect unison*.

Manufacturing Drill #1: The Major Scale

Go back to audio example ◆1. This is the scale from which you'll be manufacturing intervals. Practice singing along with it. You (and your neighbors) might prefer humming. Humming lets your ears hear your own singing better. If you're still having trouble, plug up one of your ears with your finger. You'll definitely be able to hear yourself better.

As you're singing along, visualize playing the scale with your left hand (or fretting hand) at the same time. Bassists should imagine playing the scale beginning with the second finger, guitarists should imagine starting with the second finger on the lower strings, as well as with the fourth finger on the D string.

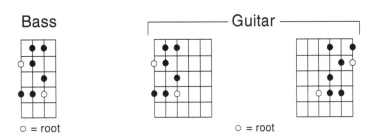

In order to reinforce the *visualization* process, let each finger contact your thumb when you imagine a fingering. (Notice that I said "imagine"—we're not picking up our instruments just yet!)

Once you're comfortable with singing the scale, practice singing along with track 2. It might be necessary to "climb the ladder" (sing the notes of the scale up to the target interval) until you get more accurate. Remember to imagine the fingering for each interval as well (make finger-thumb contact).

Manufacturing Drill #2: Major Scale Intervals

Here are ten intervals from the major scale. In each example, you'll be given the same starting pitch. Sing each interval before the answer sounds (climbing the ladder if necessary). Also, imagine the fingering for that interval. Feel free to use the "pause" button on your playback device if you need more time to sing/find the interval.

The abbreviations used for major and perfect are "ma" and "P."

3
| 1. ma3 | 2. P4 | 3. ma2 | 4. P5 | 5. ma6 |

| 6. ma2 | 7. ma7 | 8. ma3 | 9. P4 | 10. ma2 |

Do not proceed unless you're nearly perfect at creating these intervals. Each section of this book assumes that you've mastered the previous one. Jumping ahead might lead to some serious gaps in your training. (Plus, it'll make me look bad!)

The Minor Scale

While some of the intervals created from the root of the minor scale are the same as in the major scale, others are different. These will have the word *minor* in the name. Here's what the **natural minor scale** sounds like:

Here are the intervals created from the root:

1. From the root to the second note in this scale is still a **major 2nd**.

2. From the root to the third note in this scale is called a **minor 3rd**.

3. From the root to the fourth note in this scale is still a **perfect 4th**.

4. From the root to the fifth note in this scale is also still a **perfect 5th**.

5. From the root to the sixth note in this scale is called a **minor 6th**.

6. From the root to the seventh note in this scale is called a **minor 7th**.

7. From the root to the eighth note in this scale is still a **perfect octave**.

Manufacturing Drill #3: The Minor Scale

Practice singing the minor scale along with ◆. Imagine fingering the minor scale starting with the first finger for bass or for the lower strings of the guitar, and with the fourth finger for the upper strings of the guitar.

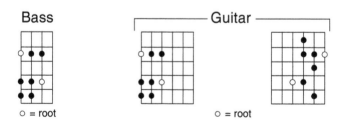

Just to make sure of your accuracy, alternate singing the minor scale ◆ and the major scale ◆. Don't forget to change fingerings.

Manufacturing Drill #4: Minor Scale Intervals

Here are ten intervals based on the minor scale. For each interval, you'll be given the same starting pitch (the root of the scale). Sing each interval before the answer is given, and imagine the fingering. "Climb the ladder" if necessary. (Use the pause button if you need more time to come up with the answer.)

The abbreviation for minor is "mi."

 1. ma2   2. mi3   3. P5   4. mi7   5. P4

        6. mi6   7. ma2   8. P8   9. mi3   10. P4

Visualization Test #1: Major Scale Intervals

Here are twelve intervals from the major scale. Each one begins from the root. Write the name of each interval that you hear, and indicate the fingering necessary to play that interval on the fingerboard diagram. The bass fingering for the major scale will start on the E string (second finger). The guitar fingerings will start on the D string (fourth finger). Guitarists should write out intervals for both fretboard diagrams.

For example, if you heard a perfect 4th, here's what your answer(s) would look like:

Bass

P4

Guitar

P4

Remember, no instruments yet.

 Bass

1. _____   2. _____   3. _____   4. _____   5. _____   6. _____

7. _____   8. _____   9. _____   10. _____   11. _____   12. _____

Guitar

1. _____   2. _____   3. _____   4. _____   5. _____   6. _____

7. _____   8. _____   9. _____   10. _____   11. _____   12. _____

Visualization Test #2: Minor Scale Intervals

Here are twelve intervals from the root of the minor scale. The bass diagrams start each interval from the E string (first finger). The guitar diagrams start from the D string (fourth finger).

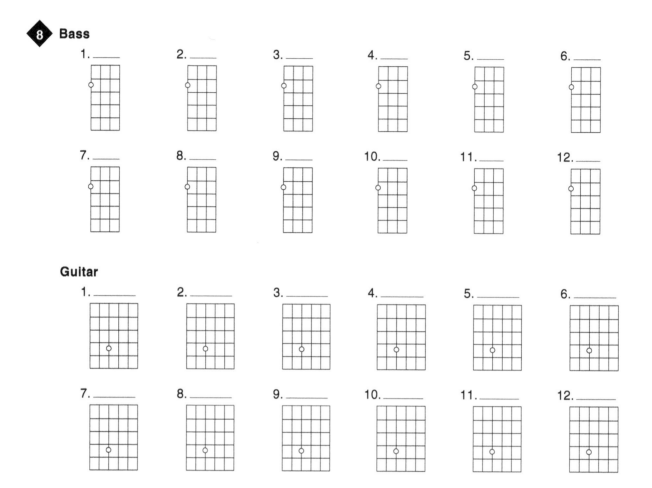

Manufacturing Tip

To improve your accuracy and confidence, try this exercise: play a major third on your instrument, but sing the minor third against it. Then switch: play a minor third, but sing the major third. Try the same thing with other intervals. Once you can nail the "other" interval, you'll never doubt what you hear.

Perfect Pitch?

Perfect pitch is the ability to recognize any note, by itself (e.g., "That's a G," "That's a B♭," etc.). It's a skill many musicians would love to have. However, even if you had perfect pitch, you'd still need to develop relative pitch, which this book is basically about. **Relative pitch** means understanding and recognizing the *relationships between notes* (e.g., "That's a minor 3rd," "That's a perfect 5th," etc.). Having perfect pitch does not necessarily mean that you comprehend those relationships. Also, perfect pitch depends on "perfect" intonation. This is a book for guitar and bass; I rest my case.

Chromatic Intervals

The rest of the intervals that happen within an octave are generally called **chromatic**. "Chromatic" music uses half step intervals. A **whole step** is the same distance as a major second (two frets). So, logically, a **half step** is the same as a minor second (one fret's distance).

A **chromatic scale** contains all twelve of the notes in an octave (in half-step increments). Here's what it sounds like.

So far, you've seen what happens to 2nds, 3rds, 6ths, and 7ths when they're modified by a half step; they become either major or minor. But what happens to 4ths and 5ths? Once again, history rears its augmented head:

- If you *lower* a 4th or 5th by a half step, it becomes **diminished**.

- If you *raise* a 4th or 5th by a half step, it becomes **augmented**.

(Since "diminished" means smaller, and "augmented" means bigger, at least it's easy to remember.)

Here are the intervals from the root to the other eleven notes of the chromatic scale. Notice that the labeling system allows some of the intervals to have more than one name. The abbreviations for diminished and augmented are "dim" and "aug."

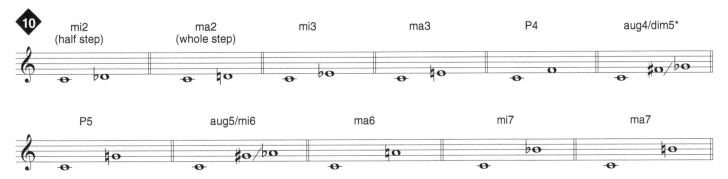

*The augmented 4th or diminished 5th is also called a **tritone**. It gets its name from the total number of whole steps in the interval: three (tri-).

Listen again to ◆9 and ◆10, visualizing these fingerings for the chromatic scale and its intervals.

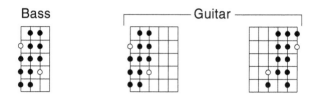

Here's a tip, especially for bassists: try to keep your hand in one position when you play through a chromatic scale, stretching your fingers to accomodate any notes that don't fall within the original four-fret area that you start with. To visualize these stretches, instead of making finger-thumb contact on these notes, simply extend your thumb out to the side (as if you were hitchhiking) to remind yourself of the stretch.

Guitarists may need to shift hand position when playing the upper octave of their instrument, but should use the same technique as the bassists for the lower octave.

Manufacturing Drill #5: Chromatic Intervals

Here are fifteen intervals from the chromatic scale. For each interval, you'll be given the same starting pitch. Sing each interval before the answer is given, and imagine the fingering. You might need to change your starting finger, depending on whether the interval comes from the major or minor scale. Pause the track if you need more time before the answer is given. Don't touch that instrument.

◆11 1. ma3   2. P5   3. mi3   4. P4   5. ma6

6. ma2   7. dim5   8. ma7   9. mi3   10. mi6

11. P4   12. ma7   13. ma6   14. ma3   15. mi2

What Goes Up Must Come Down

You may have noticed that we've only focused on ascending intervals so far. They're easier to create because we're all more familiar with building scales, triads, and chords from the root and going up. However, in the famous words of Kool & the Gang: "Get Down, Get Down." Try this exercise for descending intervals. Sing the chromatic scale descending from the root, but sing the root in between every note. You'll work your way through the scale a half step at a time while maintaining the root on top. Visualize the fingering for this as well—don't forget to use the extended thumb to remind yourself of any notes that don't fit within your initial four-fret starting area.

etc.

Once you've reached the octave below, sing your way back up the chromatic scale while still maintaining the root on top. Visualize the fingering.

Descending Tips

One thing that might make the following drills easier is knowing the equivalent *ascending* interval that a descending interval produces. Knowing this can be useful since, in the beginning, it's more difficult to remember what a descending minor 6th sounds like—if you know that the same notes can produce a major 3rd ascending, you can sing *up to the major 3rd* to remind yourself which note to sing *down an octave.*

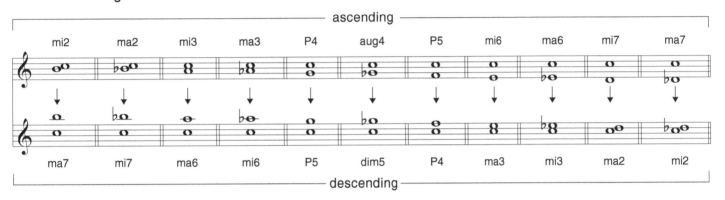

This isn't nearly as difficult as it may look at first. Notice, for instance, that every ascending/descending interval pair above adds up to the number "9." That is, a descending *2nd* produces an ascending *7th* (2+7=9); a descending *3rd* produces an ascending *6th* (3+6=9); a descending *4th* produces an ascending *5th* (4+5=9); and so on. The interval qualities are also predictable in their relationships:

major ⟷ minor

augmented ⟷ diminished

perfect ⟷ perfect

Manufacturing Drill #6: Descending Intervals

This drill focuses on descending intervals down to an augmented 4th below the root. For each interval, you'll be given the same starting pitch. Sing the interval before the answer is given, and visualize its fingering. In order to imagine the fingering, you might need to select a different finger to play the first note, depending on the interval. For instance, a major 3rd down is easier to imagine if you start from your first finger, instead of your fourth.

14   1. mi2   2. P4   3. mi3   4. ma2   5. ma3

       6. aug4   7. ma2   8. P4   9. mi3   10. mi2

Manufacturing Drill #7: More Descending Intervals

This drill focuses on descending intervals from an augmented 4th below the root to the octave below. Like #6, you'll be given the same starting pitch for each interval. Sing the interval, and visualize its fingering.

15   1. P5   2. mi6   3. ma6   4. aug4   5. mi7

       6. ma6   7. P5   8. ma7   9. mi6   10. dim5

Visualization Test #3: Even More Descending Intervals

Here are a dozen descending chromatic intervals. Indicate the interval and the fingering in the diagram. You can use your instrument soon, but not now.

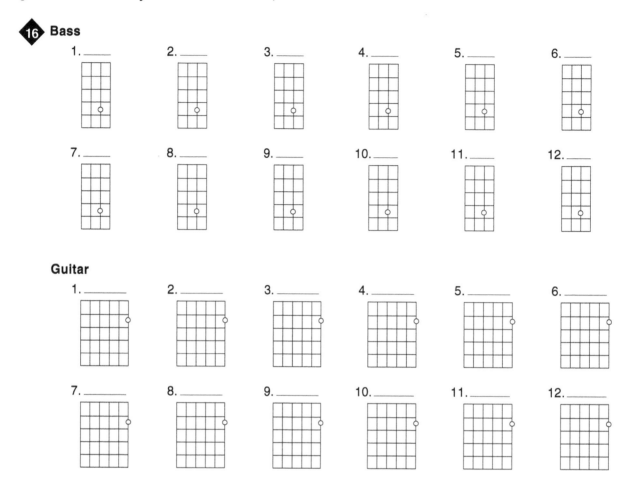

Visualization Test #4: Ascending and Descending

We're going to open this one up to ascending and descending intervals. They'll be from different notes within the same scale and octave. The scale to imagine will be one starting with the second finger on the low E string for bass and with the fourth finger on the the D string for guitar. You'll be given different starting notes, but every note you hear belongs to the same scale.

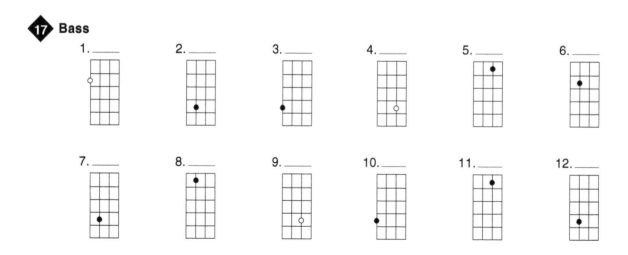

Guitar

1. _____   2. _____   3. _____   4. _____   5. _____   6. _____

7. _____   8. _____ 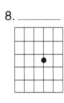   9. _____   10. _____   11. _____   12. _____

Name That Interval

Here's some interval practice that will help you see how your ears are getting along. There are thirty intervals, ascending and descending. They don't belong to any one root or scale; in fact, they jump around quite a bit. Just write the name of each interval.

1. _____	2. _____	3. _____	4. _____	5. _____	6. _____
7. _____	8. _____	9. _____	10. _____	11. _____	12. _____
13. _____	14. _____	15. _____	16. _____	17. _____	18. _____
19. _____	20. _____	21. _____	22. _____	23. _____	24. _____
25. _____	26. _____	27. _____	28. _____	29. _____	30. _____

Testing Techniques

Some of you might be familiar with using the beginning of songs to learn intervals: "Here Comes the Bride" for a perfect 4th or the "NBC" tones for a major 6th. It might be a good initial way to remember intervals and recognize them when they're played in total isolation (like on tests). However, in reality, music rarely ever happens in total isolation. Having to superimpose another melody over something you're hearing is not a method you can count on in the real world. It only works if you're trying to pass a test.

Pick Up Your Instrument (Finally!)

First of all, you've got to be in tune. Here's E–A–D–G–B–E.

Imitation Exercise #1: Follow the Leader (Major)

Now we can start to apply all that visualization stuff. This exercise is similar to the last visualization test, with notes from the C major scale only. For bass, that's the second finger, eighth fret C on the low E string; for guitar, it's the fourth finger, tenth fret C on the D string.

Bass

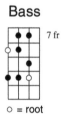

○ = root

Guitar

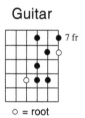

○ = root

The starting note is C. Each successive interval begins with the last note of the previous one. Play each interval after you hear it. There are twelve intervals in all. Remember to sing and visualize before you play.

Guitarists: Don't forget to try this in both positions—"guitar" and "bass".

Imitation Exercise #2: Follow the Leader (Minor)

This one is the same as before, except we'll be working from the C minor scale. That's first finger, eighth fret for bass; fourth finger, tenth fret for guitar. The starting note is C.

Bass

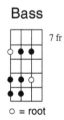

○ = root

Guitar

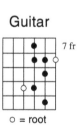

○ = root

Imitation Exercise #3: More Follow the Leader

The next three sets are not confined to any particular scale or octave, so you can expect the intervals to go anywhere. For each set, the starting note and ending note is the E-string G on the bass and the D-string G on the guitar.

Bass

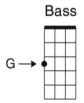

Guitar

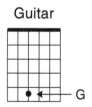

As before, each successive interval begins with the last note of the previous interval. If you find yourself hunting around for the note too much, go back and work on the manufacturing/visualization exercises to eliminate the guesswork.

Although you can use your instrument, imagining 22, 23, and 24 without it is highly recommended. For each one, the last note is the same as the first. So if you end up on the imaginary finger that you started on, mission accomplished.

Visualization Test #5: Simultaneous Intervals

By now, you should have a pretty good handle on intervals when each note is played separately. But what if the notes are played at the same time? Here are five sets of eight intervals played simultaneously. Every interval in these exercises belongs to the same single-octave major scale. From each interval to the next, only one of the notes will change at a time. The first interval is given. *Put down that instrument!*

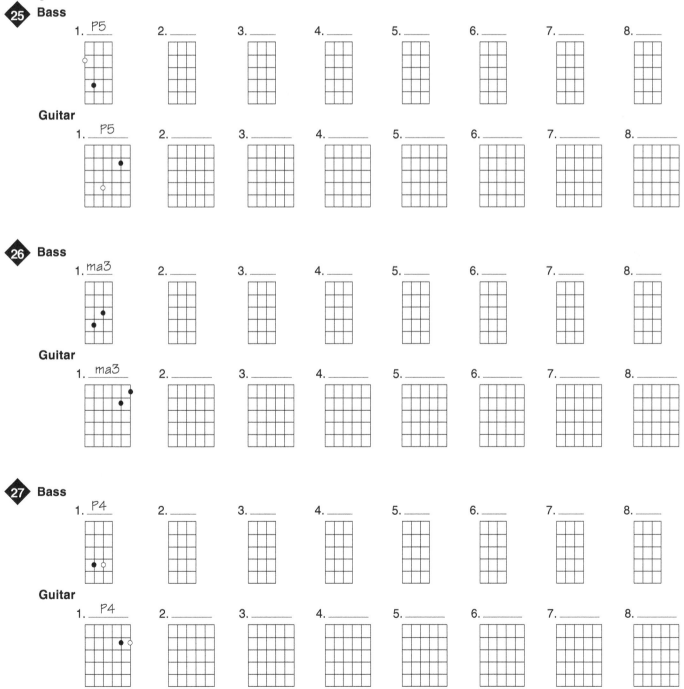

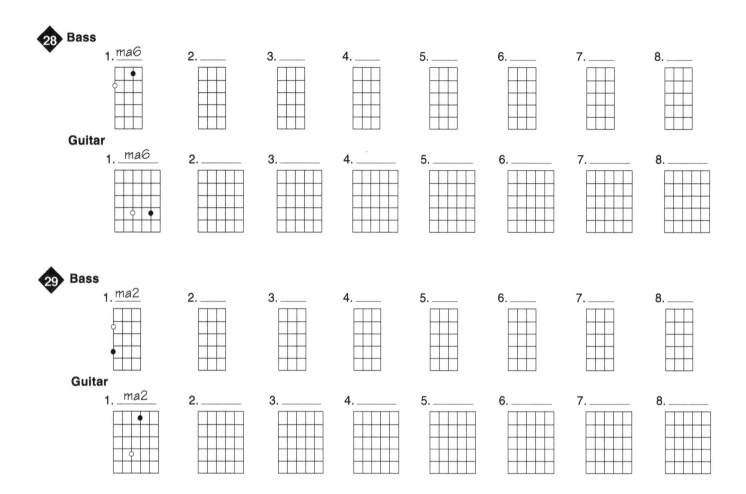

Visualization Test #6: More Simultaneous Intervals

Here are twelve more intervals played simultaneously. These intervals are *not* related to a single major scale, and both notes will change from one interval to the next. The lowest note of each interval is given. Write the name of the interval, and indicate the fingering. Remember: don't use your instrument for this.

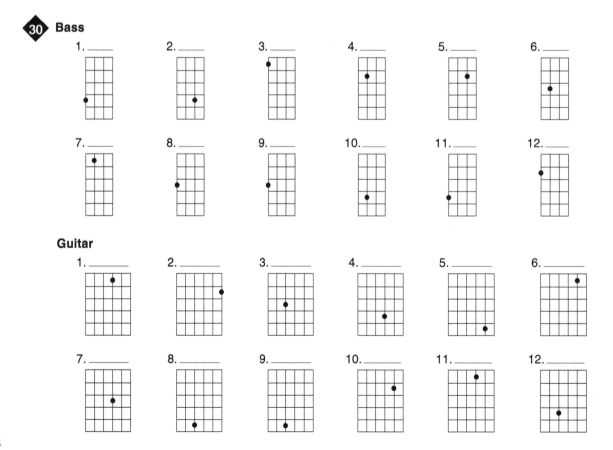

Visualization Test #7: Even More Simultaneous Intervals

Here are twelve more intervals played simultaneously. The difference here is that the note in each diagram is the *top* note of the interval. Write the name of the interval and indicate the fingering.

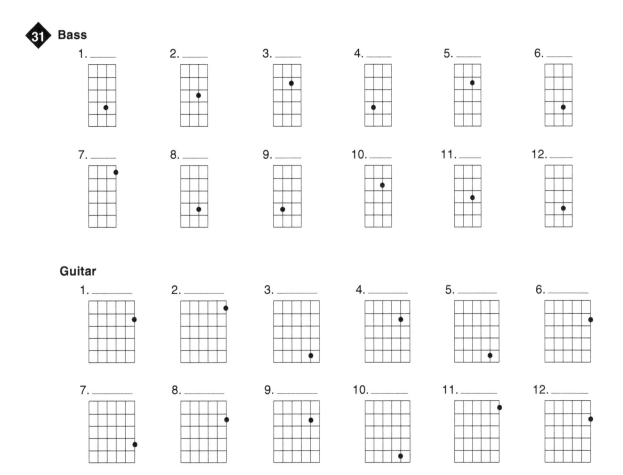

If the last three visualization tests have given you any trouble, don't be in a hurry to move on. If you're not sure about the material, take the time to back up and review. Your ear is something you can and should have total confidence in. Make sure you can "nail" each section before you move on to the next.

Triads

Now it's time to work on triads. A ***triad*** is a group of three notes stacked on top of one another. The intervals that make up a triad are thirds—which can be created by alternating every other note in a scale. Stack two thirds (major or minor in any combination), and you've got a triad. There are four kinds of triads possible. Here's how the four types can be created:

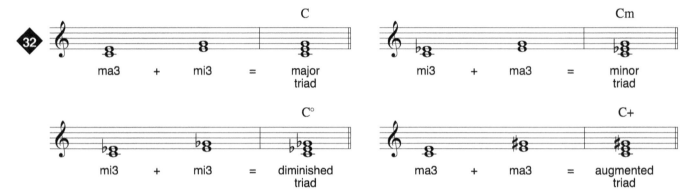

Triads are made up of a root, 3rd, and 5th. Since major and minor triads both have a perfect 5th, they are labeled by the kind of 3rd that they have. Diminished and augmented triads, on the other hand, are labeled by the kind of 5th that they use.

Manufacturing Drill #8: Movable Triads

Here's one where your instrument can help you out (if you need it). Find a pitch that's in the lower part of your singing register. From that pitch, sing the four types of triads in this order: augmented, major, minor, and diminished. Notice that, in this order, you only need to change one note at a time to get to the next triad. Use your instrument to check your singing and to help you out, if necessary:

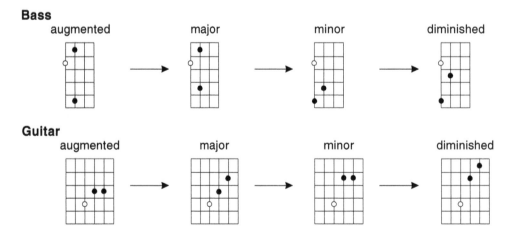

Sing through the four types at least a couple of times this way, then move up a half step and do the same thing. Once you've done that, move down a whole step for the four triads. Then move back to where you started (up one half step), and repeat the whole process until you're able to create the triads without your instrument. With or without your instrument, you should be visualizing the triad shapes (making finger-thumb contact) as you sing them.

More Triad Fingerings

Repeat Manufacturing Drill #8, visualizing these alternate triad fingerings. The bass fingerings can be applied to either of the bottom two strings. The guitar fingerings will work only from the G string.

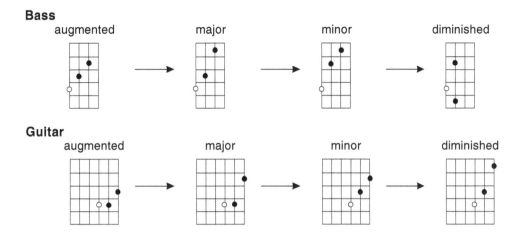

Manufacturing Drill #9: Ancient Triad Sequence Puzzle

Find a starting pitch in the middle of your singing register, and play it on your instrument. By accurately singing the following series of triads, you'll end up on the same note from which you started. Begin each successive triad with the last note of the previous triad—i.e., the 5th of each triad becomes root of the next one. You'll occasionally need to drop down an octave to keep the triads in your singing range. The 5th of the last triad will be the root of the first triad you started on. Only use your instrument to check your first and last note.

Triad sequences:

1) minor–augmented–major–minor–major

2) major–minor–augmented–major–minor

3) augmented–diminished–major–augmented–minor

4) diminished–augmented–minor–augmented–major

Visualization Test #8: Simultaneous Triads

Here are twelve triads played simultaneously. (The notes of each triad are played simultaneously, not all twelve triads at once—that would make things difficult to say the least.) All you have to do is identify the *kind* of triad. Eliminate the guesswork by singing each triad (don't use your instrument). Often, the first note that your voice will be able to sing will be the highest note. The test for a root of a triad is if you can sing two consecutive thirds from that note. What if thirds don't work? From the 5th of a triad to the root above it (where the triad starts over) is a perfect 4th. If you can sing a perfect 4th from your note, you've located the 5th and the root (the higher of the two).

🔹33 1. _____   2. _____   3. _____   4. _____   5. _____   6. _____

7. _____   8. _____   9. _____   10. _____   11. _____   12. _____

Visualization Test #9: More Simultaneous Triads

Here are twelve more triads played simultaneously. They all have the same note in common. You'll hear that note before each triad is played. From that note, you can determine (by singing) whether it's the root, 3rd, or 5th, and what type of triad it is. Indicate the type of triad and its fingering.

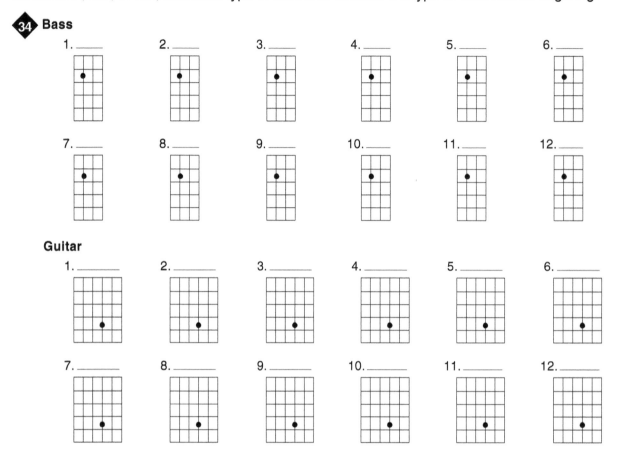

Imitation Exercise #4: Triad Progressions

Here are four progressions that use triads. Each progression lasts for four measures and repeats once. The bass and guitar parts are in unison. There's one triad per measure (four different triads). Don't start playing right away. Instead, sing along with the audio while imagining the notes on the fingerboard. You may need to break each progression down, focusing on one aspect at a time:

- Sing the root notes only of each triad, and identify the intervals between them.
- Listen for the quality of each triad, and visualize their fingerings.

Once you've got a good idea of how to play a progression, pick up your instrument. If you find that you're fishing around on the neck for the notes too much, back up several pages and spend some more time on the visualization tests. The starting pitch for each progression is shown.

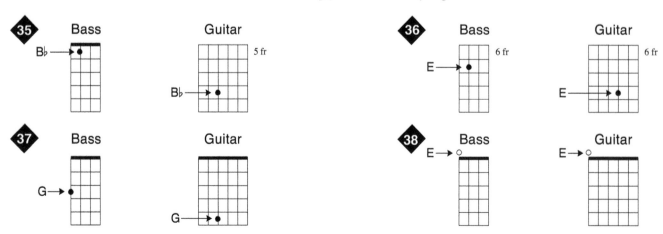

First Inversion

A chord or triad that has its root as the lowest note is in **root position**. When a note other than the root is the lowest note, it's an **inversion**. For example, when you put the root up an octave, the 3rd becomes the lowest note, and you get **first inversion**. Here's what the four types of triads sound like when inverted. You'll hear each triad in root position, then in first inversion:

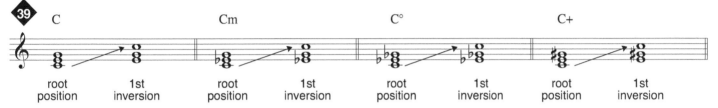

C	Cm	C°	C+
root position	1st inversion	root position	1st inversion	root position	1st inversion	root position	1st inversion

Manufacturing Drill #10: First Inversion

This one is exactly like Manufacturing Drill #8 except that you're singing 3–5–1 instead of 1–3–5. Find a pitch in the lower part of your singing register. From that pitch, sing the four types of triads (augmented, major, minor, and diminished), visualizing their fingerings as you do. Use your instrument to check your singing and to help you out, if necessary.

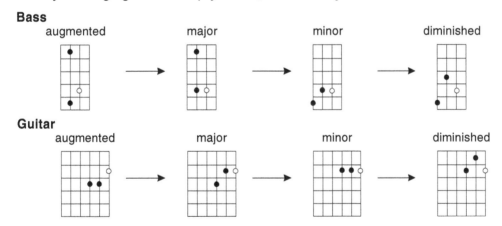

Sing the four triads in inversion, then start the triads a half step above where you began, and then a whole step below that. Don't move on until you can sing/imagine the triads without your instrument.

Manufacturing Drill #11: Descending First Inversion

This time, find a pitch that's in the upper part of your singing register. From that pitch, sing the four types of first inversion triads descending: 1–5–3. Essentially, you'll be singing down a fourth, and then a third, for each triad:

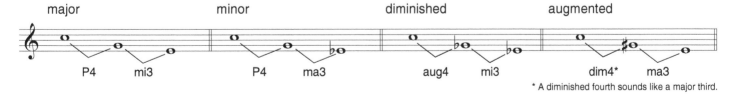

major	minor	diminished	augmented
P4 mi3	P4 ma3	aug4 mi3	dim4* ma3

* A diminished fourth sounds like a major third.

Sing the four triads in inversion, then start the triads a half step above where you began, and then a whole step below that.

More First Inversion Fingerings

Repeat Manufacturing Drills #10 and 11, visualizing these alternate first-inversion fingerings. The bass fingerings can begin on either of the top two strings. The guitar fingerings will work only from the B string.

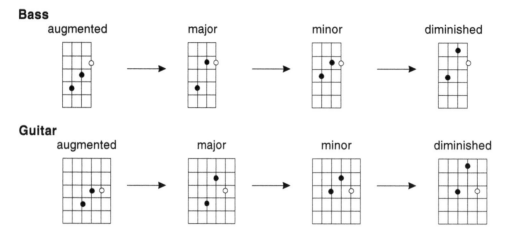

Visualization Test #10: Simultaneous Triads

Here are twelve triads played simultaneously. They're in either root position or first inversion (you decide). The highest note is given. Use that note to determine (by singing) whether it's the root, 3rd, or 5th and what type of triad it is. Indicate the type of triad (with inversion, if necessary) and the fingering for each triad.

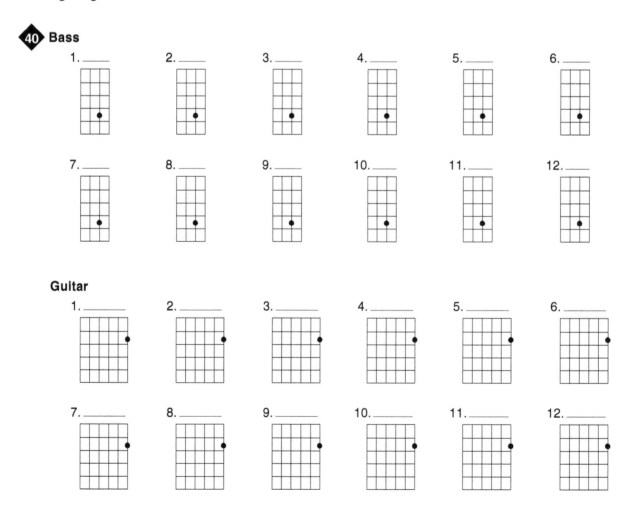

Visualization Test #11: More Simultaneous Triads

Here are twelve more triads played simultaneously. These all have the same middle note in common. As in Visualization Test #10, use that note to identify the type of triad and indicate the inversion and fingering. Remember, singing each triad will eliminate the guesswork.

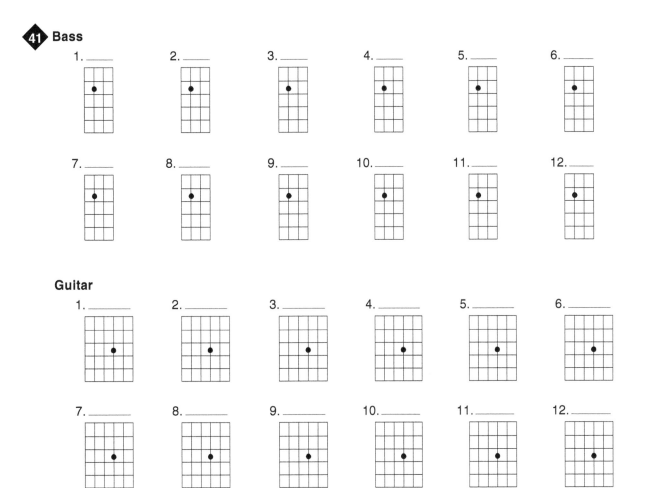

Second Inversion

If you put the root and the 3rd up an octave you get *second inversion*. The 5th becomes the lowest note. Here's what the four types of triads sound like inverted. You'll hear each triad in root position, first inversion, then second inversion:

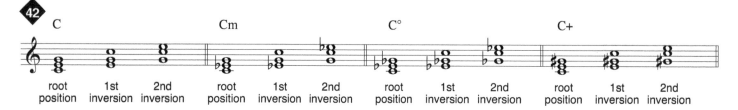

Manufacturing Drill #12: Second Inversion

This one is like Manufacturing Drills #8 and #10 except that you're singing 5–1–3. Find a pitch in the lower part of your singing register. From that pitch, sing the four types of triads, then sing the same triads a half step up, and a whole step below that. Use your instrument to check yourself, if necessary:

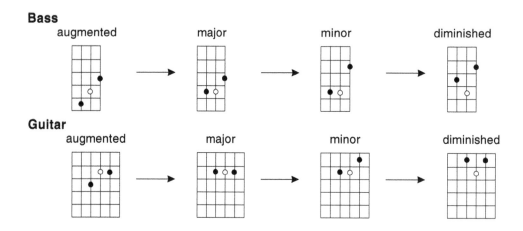

Remember, the interval from the 5th up to the root is *some kind of fourth*. For major and minor, you start out by singing a perfect fourth. For diminished and augmented triads, you start out with opposite intervals: an augmented fourth for the diminished triad, a diminished fourth for the augmented triad.

More Second Inversion Fingerings

Repeat Manufacturing Drill #12, visualizing these alternate second inversion fingerings. The bass fingerings are not quite as comfortable, but they can be applied to any of the bottom three strings. The guitar fingerings will work only from the high E string.

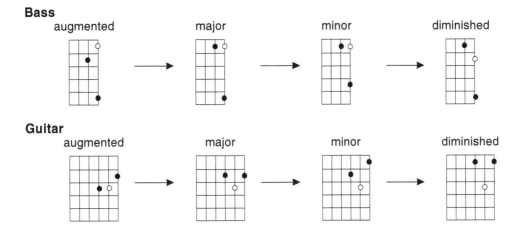

Bass
augmented   major   minor   diminished

Guitar
augmented   major   minor   diminished

Manufacturing Drill #13: The Mother of All Triad Drills

Here's the ultimate (and final, woo-hoo!) triad manufacturing drill. Start with a pitch in the lower part of your singing register. From that pitch, sing the following twelve triads:

> Root position: augmented—major—minor—diminished
>
> First inversion: augmented—major—minor—diminished
>
> Second inversion: augmented—major—minor—diminished

Your starting pitch for this drill should remain constant, whether you're singing root position, first inversion, or second inversion—which means the chord roots may change from one inversion to the next.

O.K. It wasn't completely final. (So sue me.) Sing the same twelve triads descending from a note in the upper part of your register.

Don't forget to visualize the chord shapes.

Visualization Test #12: 10 Triad Types

Here are ten triads from one note. Each triad will start with the same note. Indicate the fingering, the kind of triad, and inversion (if necessary). Don't use your instrument.

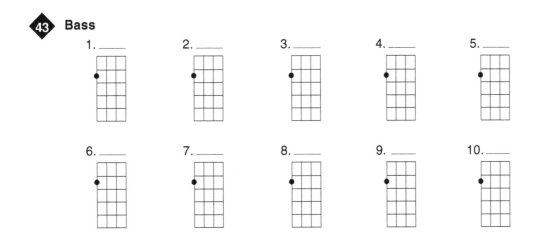

43 **Bass**

1. _____   2. _____   3. _____   4. _____   5. _____

6. _____   7. _____   8. _____   9. _____   10. _____

Guitar

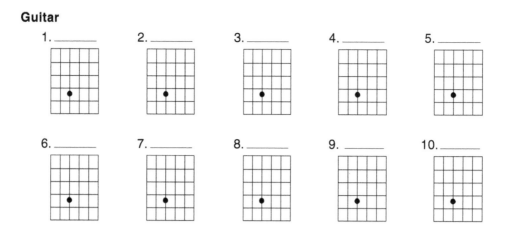

Visualization Test #13: 12 Simultaneous Triad Types

Here are twelve more triads played simultaneously. They all have the same note in common, but it's not always the lowest note. You'll hear the common note before each triad is played. Indicate the fingering, the type of triad, and inversion (if necessary). No instruments.

44 Bass

Guitar

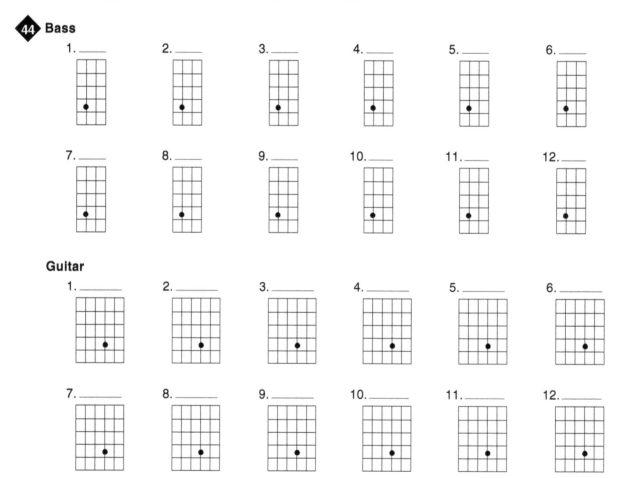

Imitation Exercise #5: Follow the Leader

O.K. Now use your instrument to follow the triads around. The next three exercises use ascending and descending triads in all of the inversions we've studied so far. Each triad begins with the last note of the previous triad. There's enough time between triads to do the following: sing and then visualize each triad before you try to play it. If you're guessing or hunting around for notes, it's time go back, review, and prepare yourself better. So that you can check yourself, each exercise begins and ends on the same note: G. (This is the first note of the first triad and the last note of the last triad.) Try starting these first in the position shown, then, when you're ready, try transposing them to different octaves on your instrument. Don't forget to use the extended thumb to remind yourself of any notes that don't fit within your initial four-fret starting area.

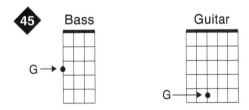

Imitation Exercise #6: Triad Progressions

Here are three progressions based on triads. Each progression lasts for eight measures, with one triad per measure, and repeats. The bass and guitar parts are in unison. Again, don't start playing right away; listen to the whole progression. Then, since these are longer progressions, try to follow the starting (lowest) note for each triad. Once you've got the starting notes, then concentrate on the triad qualities. Try singing along, imagining the notes on the fingerboard. The starting note for each progression is given.

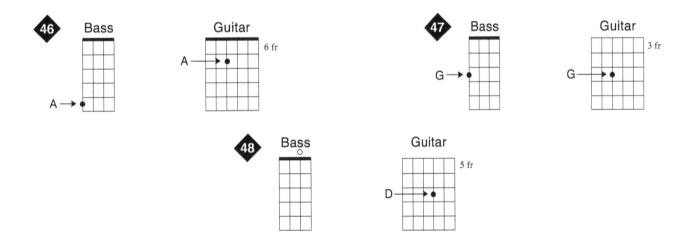

Melodic Shapes

One word that strikes dread into most guitar and bass students is "sightsinging." (Go ahead, roll your eyes back.) So far, it's been disguised as "Manufacturing Drills." I suppose it could be further disguised by calling it "internal melodic creation" or something like that, but you may as well face the fact that sightsinging is part of what you have to do to become a better musician, just like in a legit music school. (Since you're working from this book, at least you don't have to attend 7:30 a.m. sightsinging classes like I did.) The next few Manufacturing Drills (you know what we're talking about) will use regular treble and bass clef notation to get you to create *melodic shapes*. These shapes use a combination of intervals that we've studied so far but don't necessarily fit into any triad or chord descriptions.

Manufacturing Drill #13: Diatonic Melodic Shapes

By now, you should be quite proficient at identifying, singing, and visualizing scales and their intervals. With that in mind, here are twenty sets of three-note melodic shapes in treble clef (for guitar) and bass clef (uh, for bass), all from the same starting note. The starting note will be the root of either a major or minor scale, and the notes will all come from that scale. First, spend some time on these *without* the audio; for each example, identify the scale, visualize the shape, and sing the intervals. Then, once you've got that down, listen to the audio to check yourself. Sing along with the cheesy choir, and you'll feel just like you're in ear-training class. Instruments? No!

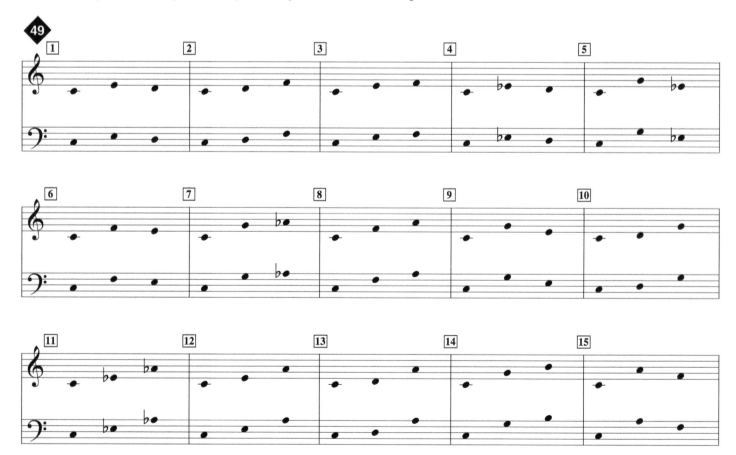

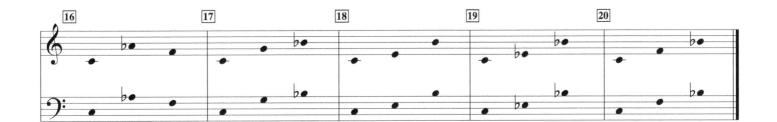

Manufacturing Drill #14: Chromatic Melodic Shapes

Here are twenty more three-note melodic shapes in treble and bass clef, all from the same starting note. This time, the notes won't belong to any particular scale and will include more descending intervals. This will be a bit tougher. Again, spend as much time as you need on this *without* the audio. Visualize and sing each one, then do it again. Once you feel comfortable with your singing, check it against the audio. Instr... No!

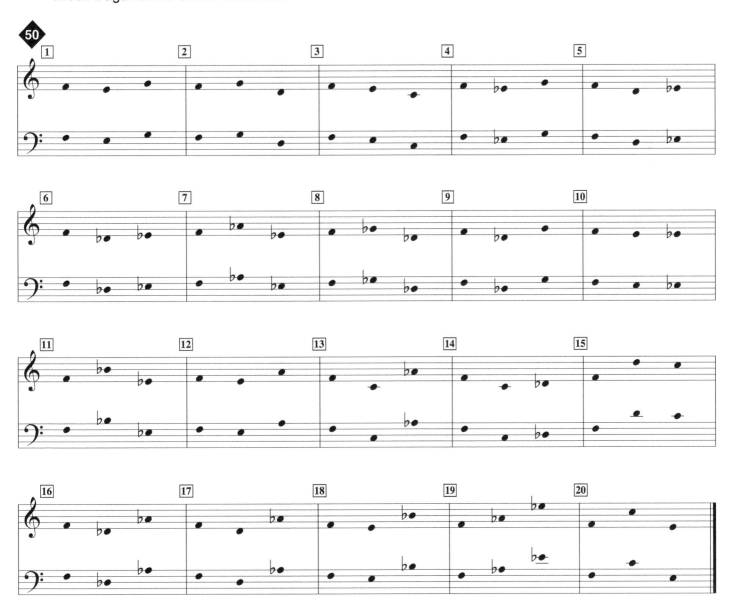

Manufacturing Drill #15: More Diatonic Melodic Shapes

These involve four-note melodic shapes. There are twenty in treble and bass clef from the same starting note. Just like Drill #13, the starting note is the root of a major or minor scale and the notes will come from that scale. You know the routine; do it without the audio first. Ins... No!

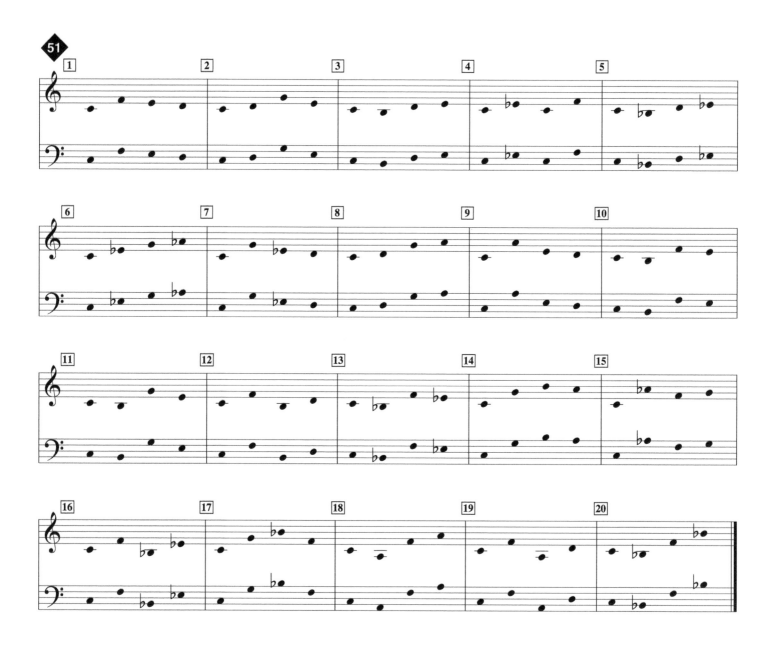

Manufacturing Drill #16: More Chromatic Melodic Shapes

Here are twenty more four-note melodic shapes. These all start from the same note but don't necessarily belong to the same key..

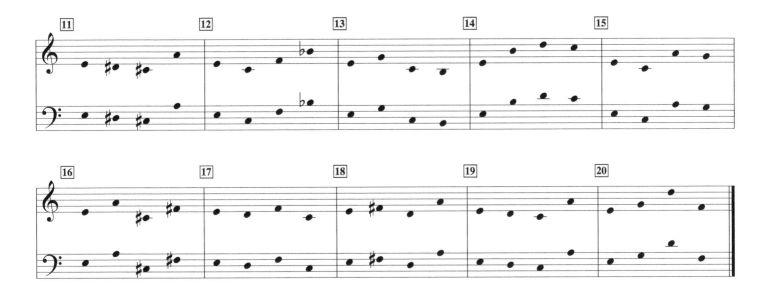

Visualization Test #14: Four-Note Diatonic Shapes

Since I've revealed the true identity of the Manufacturing Drills ("sightsinging"), you might as well know that the following Visualization Tests are actually called "melodic dictation." Listen to the following four-note melodies, and write the answers on the staff. The starting note is the root of the major or minor key that the rest of the notes belong to. It may help you to visualize the shapes first—even make your own fretboard diagrams if you need to. In… Not yet!

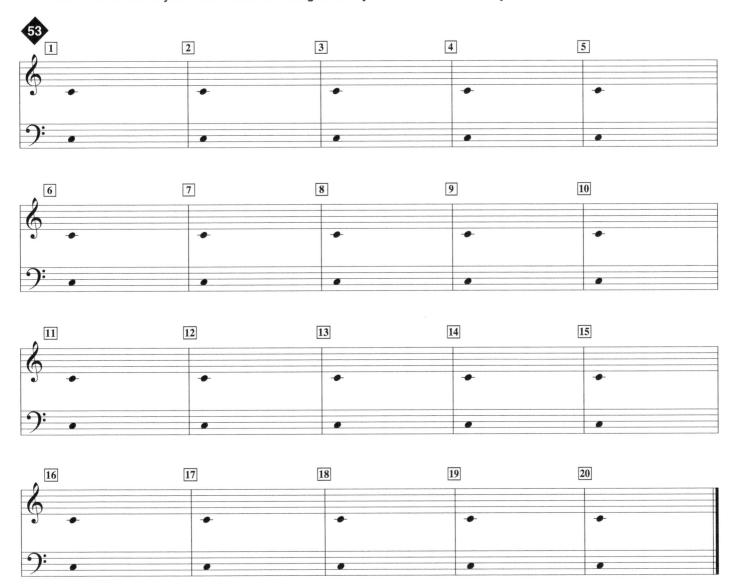

Visualization Test #15: Four-Note Chromatic Shapes

These four-note melodies all start with the same note but don't belong to any particular key. Visualize the shapes and write the answers on the staff. Your basses and guitars are gathering dust, right?

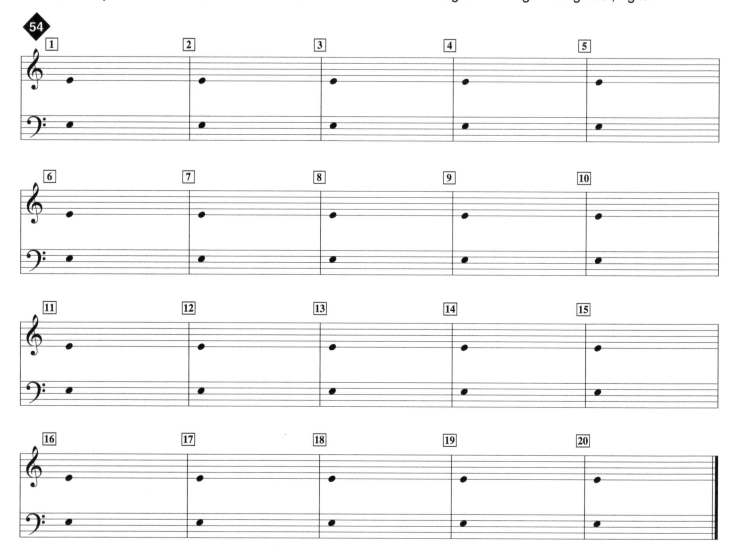

Imitation Exercise #7: Follow the Leader

Surprise: the legit music schools don't have the equivalent of imitation exercises, so we're on our own. For the next two, you'll hear the idea and then its repetition. Listen to the idea, then play along when it's repeated. (That's right, use your instrument.) Notice that the last note of each three-note idea becomes the first note of the next. Also notice that the first and last note of each exercise are the same.

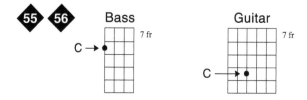

Imitation Exercise #8: The Leader's Got Rhythm

Here are two more just like Imitation Exercise #7, but they don't all have the same rhythmic value.

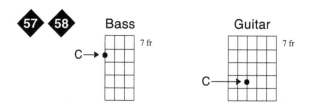

Rhythms

If you ever plan on reading music, or writing your own, you need to become familiar with **rhythm**. Rhythmic notation basically involves indicating when a note happens and how long it lasts.

Most music is based on a regular pulse. In notation, that pulse—or the "beats" of that pulse—is grouped into bars, or **measures**, which are separated from one other by **bar lines**.

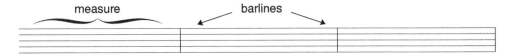

Each measure contains a consistent number of beats. The most common number of beats per measure is four. The most common beat value is a quarter note (1/4 of a measure). Those two pieces of information (the number of beats in a measure and the value of those beats) are what you see at the beginning of a piece of music, in the **time signature**:

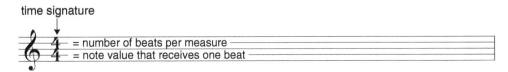

4/4 means four quarter notes per measure. Because it is the most common time signature, 4/4 is also called **common time**. It's the only time signature we'll be using in this book, but it's by no means the only one you'll run across in your musical experiences. Here are some of the most frequently used time signatures:

Here are the basic symbols for the durations of a note, along with their equivalent rests. (A rest is a silence, when no note is played.)

Symbol	Name	Number per measure of 4/4	Rest
o	whole note	o 1 per measure	▬
♩ (half)	half note	2 per measure	▬
♩	quarter note	4 per measure	𝄽
♪	eighth note	8 per measure	𝄾
♬	sixteenth note	16 per measure	𝄿

A *tie* is used to join notes together to create a longer value

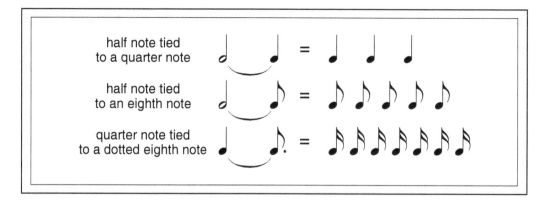

A *dot* beside a note extends its duration by 1/2. For example, a half note's length is two quarter notes; a dotted half note's length is three quarter notes. This works for rests as well.

Notation Demo

Here are two examples of music that demonstrate rhythmic notation. Notice how the notation tells you where the notes happen in relation to the quarter-note pulse in the background. Practice tapping the rhythms along with the examples. The count-off is four beats.

Rhythmic Dictation

No euphemisms here. Listen to the rhythm, write the rhythm, be the rhythm. Don't worry about the durations; just notate where you hear the attacks of the cowbell notes.

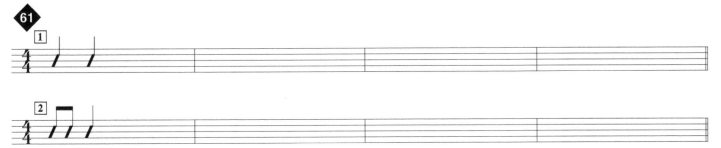

More Rhythmic Dictation

Be careful; these examples use sixteenth notes.

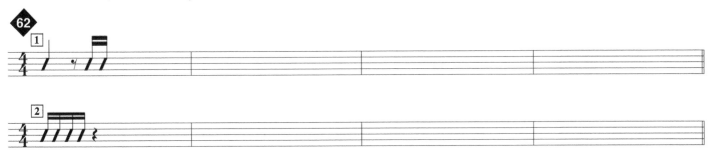

Imitation Exercise #9: Diatonic Rhythms

These ten examples all belong to a single key and start and end with the same note. For bass and guitar, it'll be the F located on the A string, eighth fret, second finger. Sing the intervals and rhythms before you strap on your instrument and try to play them. Each one will be played twice. Play along the second time.

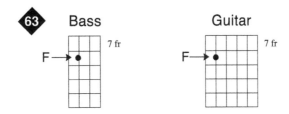

Imitation Exercise #10: Chromatic Rhythms

These ten examples also start and end with the same note. For bass, it's the B♭ located on the D string, eighth fret, fourth finger, and for guitar it's the B♭ located on the high E string, sixth fret, second finger. These do not stick to a single key; they are chromatic. Sing the intervals and rhythms before you try to play them.

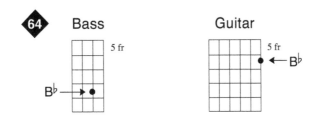

Music Transcription #1: Guitar and Bass Lines

Here are three examples of guitar, bass, and drums all playing at once (what a concept!). The starting notes for bass and guitar are given. The examples are four-measure phrases that repeat, so you'll get to hear each one a few times. Use your instrument and some spare manuscript paper if you think you'll be erasing too much. Better yet, transcribe it without your instrument.

Hint: the first note of the bass part is often the key that the music will be in, though not in every case (as you will see here).

10 Seventh Chords

Seventh chords are created just like triads, by stacking thirds (every other note of a scale) on top of one another. Add one more third on top of a triad, and you've got a seventh chord. The name "seventh" comes from the interval between the chord's bottom and top notes.

Here are the four main kinds of seventh chords:

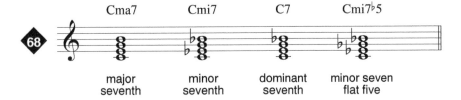

They're all labeled by what kind of 3rd and 7th they have. The two exceptions are the "7" and the "mi7♭5." The "7" is called "dominant seventh"—because it rules, dude. Actually, it has something to do with how the dissonant-sounding interval between the 3rd and the 7th (the tritone) typically resolves to the root and 3rd of the tonic chord—but that'll never win you any money on "Jeopardy." The "minor seven flat five" describes itself perfectly: a minor seventh chord with a flatted 5th.

Manufacturing Drill #17: Seventh Chords

Déjà vu: Find a pitch that's in the lower part of your singing register. From that pitch, sing the four types of seventh chords, in this order: major seventh, dominant seventh, minor seventh, and minor seven flat five. Just like with the triads, this order allows you to change only one note to get to the next chord. Use your instrument to check your singing and to help you out, if necessary.

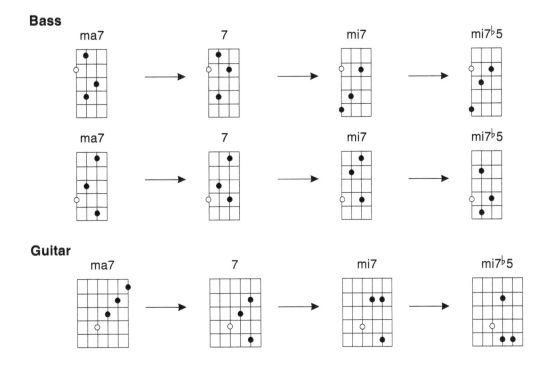

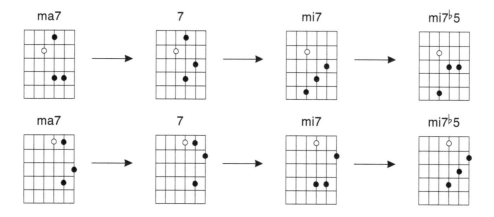

Sing through the four types at least a couple of times, move up a half step and do the same thing, move down a whole step for the four chords, then move back to where you started (up a half step) and repeat the whole process until you're able to create the seventh chords without your instrument.

Manufacturing Drill #18: Seventh Chords Descending

Find a pitch in the upper part of your singing register, and sing the four types of seventh chords descending. Sing down from the root (1–7–5–3–1), and move your starting root around as in previous drills. Visualize these too.

Visualization Test #17: Simultaneous Seventh Chords

Here are ten seventh chords in root position, all beginning from the same root. No instruments. You know what to do:

- Sing the chord
- Identify its quality
- Visualize its shape on the fretboard

Once you've sung the root for the first chord, remember it; you can use it to help yourself sing and identify the remaining chords. (Given that there's only one root here, there are only so many possibilities.)

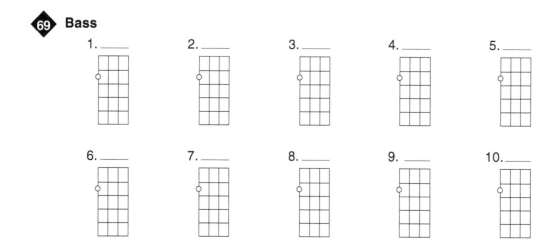

Guitar

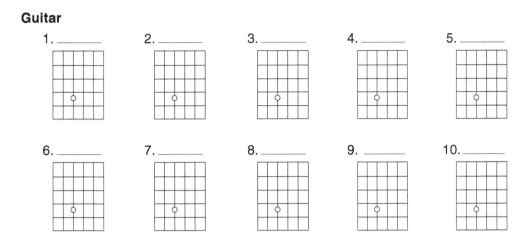

Seventh Chord Inversions

Seventh chord inversions are not that much different from triad inversions. Seventh chords in first inversion and second inversion have the 3rd and 5th as their lowest notes, respectively—just like triads. However, with seventh chords there is also a **third inversion,** which has a 7th as the lowest note.

Look at it this way: a root position seventh chord is created with three consecutive thirds. Seventh chord inversions involve putting the root and other chord tones up an octave higher, which results in the interval of a second between the 7th and the root (on octave up). You can create a first inversion seventh chord by stacking two thirds then a second: 3–5–7–1. Second inversion can be created by stacking a third, a second, then a third: 5–7–1–3. Third inversion can be created by stacking a second then two thirds: 7–1–3–5.

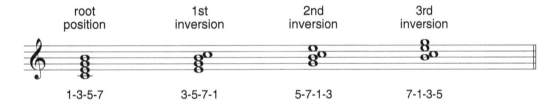

Manufacturing Drill #19: Seventh Chord Inversions

Go back to that low starting pitch. Sing the four types of seventh chords in first inversion (3–5–7–1), then second inversion (5–3–7–1), and then third inversion (7–1–3–5). Easy, isn't it? Use your instrument... Not!

FIRST INVERSION
Bass

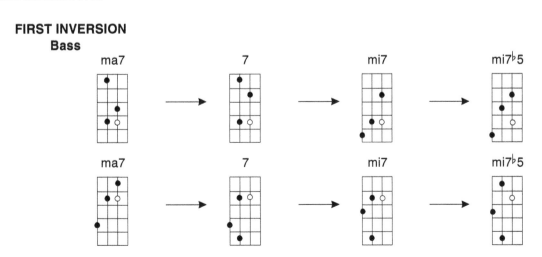

Guitar

ma7 → 7 → mi7 → mi7♭5

ma7 → 7 → mi7 → mi7♭5

or → or → or

SECOND INVERSION
Bass

ma7 → 7 → mi7 → mi7♭5

ma7 → 7 → mi7 → mi7♭5

Guitar

ma7 → 7 → mi7 → mi7♭5

ma7 → 7 → mi7 → mi7♭5

THIRD INVERSION
Bass

ma7 → 7 → mi7 → mi7♭5

ma7 → 7 → mi7 → mi7♭5

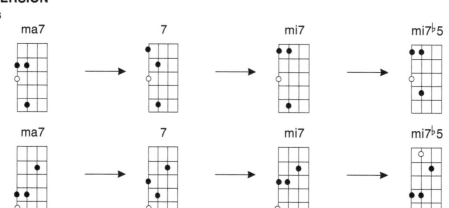

Guitar

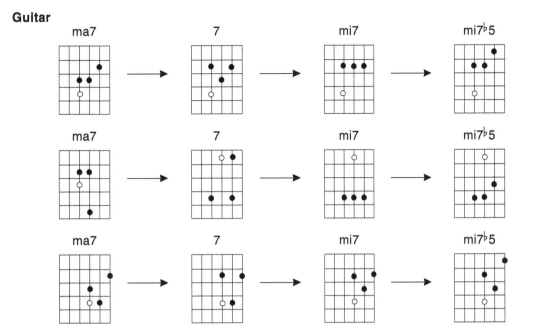

| ma7 | 7 | mi7 | mi7♭5 |

Visualization Test #16: Seventh Chord Inversions

Here are twelve seventh chords. Some of them could be inverted. They all start with the same note. Don't use your instrument. Take your time with each of these.

- Sing the chord
- Identify its quality
- Identify its inversion
- Visualize its shape

 Bass

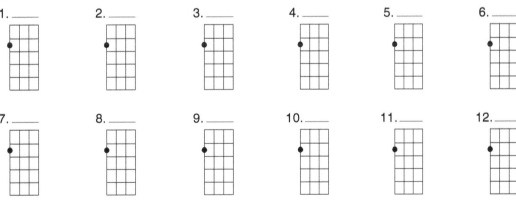

Guitar

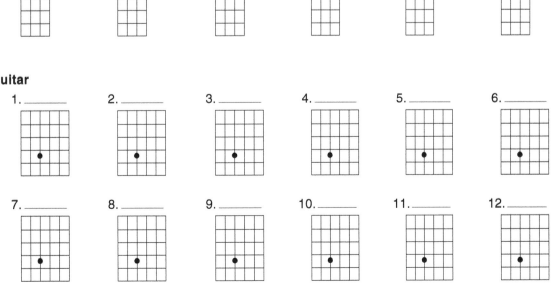

Visualization Test #18: Simultaneous Seventh Chords Inverted For Your Listening Pleasure

Here are twenty seventh chords. The first ten all share the same lowest note (it won't be the root). The last ten all share the same highest note, also not the root. Don't forget to pause the audio for more time. Don't you just love inversion? (Put down that gun—I mean, instrument.)

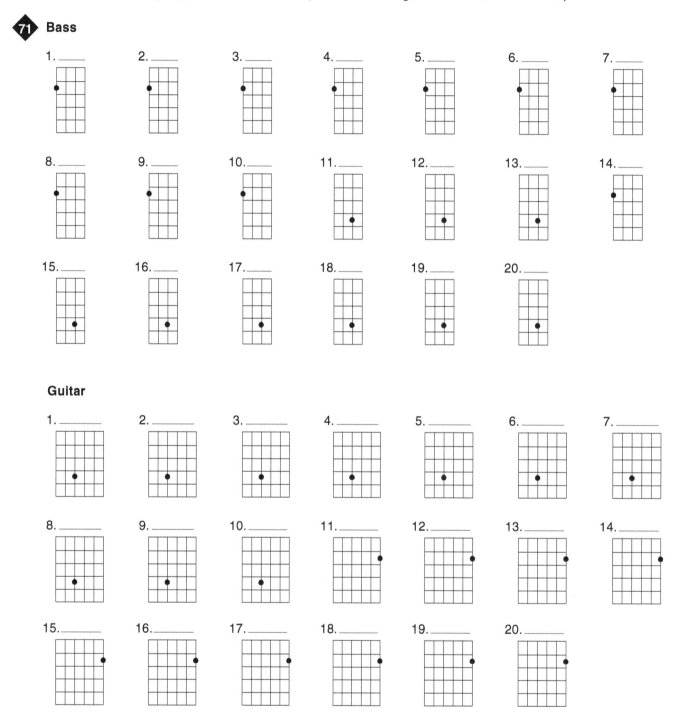

Seventh Chord Tip

If you had trouble with the last one, you're not alone. As I mentioned before, most people automatically sing the highest note of any chord they hear. Trouble is, that's not usually the root. The test for a root of a seventh chord is if you can sing three consecutive thirds from it. If your note doesn't pass the test, then it's fairly simple to find the root. First of all, sing thirds until they don't work. Once you find that a third doesn't work from a note, then try singing some kind of second. Remember, an inverted seventh chord will have the distance of a major or minor second from 7 to 1. Once you find that second, then you've found 7 to 1.

Seventh Chord Progressions

Here are the diatonic seventh chords built from the notes in a major scale:

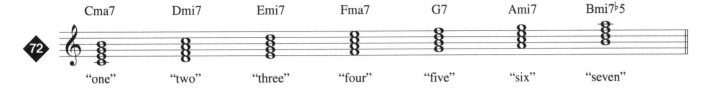

Because the intervals between the notes of a major scale are fixed, the kind of seventh chord created from each note of the scale is consistent from one major key to the next (anything from A major to Z major). This has led to convenient abbreviations for the names of the chords: "the one chord," "the two chord," "the three chord," etc. Each abbreviation implies that you know the quality of that kind of chord. For example, what's the "five" chord in A♭ major? E♭7, of course.

Manufacturing Drill #20: Seventh Chord Progressions

Sing the following seventh chord progressions, using whatever inversion is necessary to keep all the notes of the chords within an octave. For example, "one–four–two–five" would look and sound like this (in C):

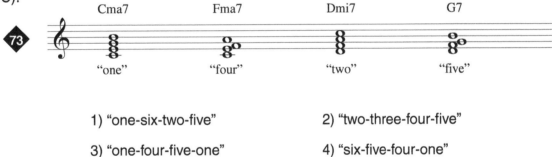

    1) "one-six-two-five"   2) "two-three-four-five"

    3) "one-four-five-one"   4) "six-five-four-one"

Now sing the same progressions with descending arpeggios. For example:

Seventh Chord Statistics

Since we're dealing with a consistent set of chords from key to key, the relationships between those chords can sometimes be used to determine the key center for different sets of chord changes. Knowing the key center is helpful sometimes when you're transcribing music, as there are tendencies that progressions tend to follow that are easier to predict and identify if you know the key center. If you are trying to identify a key center, there are certain chords, or combinations of chords, that will tell you what key you're in:

The dominant seventh

Since it only occurs diatonically as the "five" chord in a major key, the dominant seventh chord can tell you the key center all by itself. Unfortunately, exceptions to this in real music are numerous, especially in blues progressions where most of the chords are dominant.

Two major seventh chords a fourth apart

Major seventh chords occur on the root and the 4th scale degrees in a major key. For example, B♭ma7 and E♭ma7 tell you that you're in the key of B♭.

Two minor seventh chords a whole step apart

There are three locations for minor seventh chords: "two," "three," and "six." Since "two" and "three" are a whole step apart, if you find these, you've found the root. For example, Gmi7 and Ami7 tell you that you're in the key of F.

Minor seventh with a major seventh one half step up

The only place that a minor seventh is adjacent to a major seventh is from the "three" chord to the "four" chord. For example, Bmi7 and Cma7 tell you that you're in the key of G.

Music Transcription #2: Seventh Chords in a Key

Here are five progressions that use seventh chords in root position. They have four chords each, and they're diatonic. You're given the root of the first chord. Use your instrument only if you have to. The voicings (1–3–5–7) are spread to give a more realistic effect and more musical voice leading. The result might be 1–7–3–5, but as long as you identify and sing from the root, you'll be O.K. Transcribe the progressions in this order:

1. Identify the root movement.
   Indicate the letter name of the root on the line for each chord (e.g., <u>A</u>).

2. Identify the chord quality.
   Next to the root, put the chord symbol (e.g., <u>Ami7</u>).

3. Use the seventh chord statistics to help you identify the major key center that all four chords belong to.

For example:

◆ 75	G				key center
	Gma7	Ami7	Bmi7	Cma7	G / key center

◆ 76	D				key center

◆ 77	C				key center

◆ 78	B♭				key center

◆ 79	G				key center

◆ 80	A				key center

Music Transcription #3: Seventh Chords in a Key with Inversions

These five progressions use seventh chords, and some of them are inverted. Like the previous five, the chord voicings are spread apart. The first voicing is given. Write the rest of the voicings on the staff paper and indicate the chord symbol. If a chord is inverted, write its regular label, a slash, and then the note that's in the bass, e.g., A♭ma/C.

These may be quite a challenge, so here are a few tips:

- Listen for the outer voices (the bass and the top note) and notate those first. They're usually the easiest notes to pick out.
- Listen for the quality of each chord; it may help you figure out the middle voices.
- Don't just think of these progressions as chords; think of them as four simultaneous melodic lines. Each line moves very smoothly, often stepwise, and never makes a leap larger than a third.

Again, take your time with these. Instruments? O.K.

Imitation Exercise #11: More Melodic Shapes

Hopefully, as you've worked your way through this book, you've gotten better at being able to play what you hear. Here's some more work in that direction. These are four- and five-note melodic shapes. They happen over an eighth-note rhythm section groove. Each melody is repeated with a very brief pause in between. Listen to the melody, sing and visualize it, then play along with the repetition. (You may want to listen to this a few times before you actually pick up your instrument.) Each idea fits musically with the bass note groove, so it's up to you to find the starting note.

Imitation Exercise #12: More Advanced Melodic Shapes

This one's similar to Imitation Exercise #11, except the rhythms and intervals are a little more adventurous. Also, the melodies are longer.

Transcribing Tips

How you operate the controls of your playback device can have a big impact on your ability to transcribe. That's right, you need to develop "chops" on your playback device. If you're focusing on an idea but rewind too far, then you have to wait and listen to a bunch of extra information that can interfere with your concentration. Learn to hold down the rewind button just long enough that you can start right before the idea you're focusing on. Even more important is learning how to "stop on a dime." Even the fastest riff can be broken down and transcribed if you can consistently stop on the right notes. Instead of trying to listen all the way through a complex line, break it up into two or maybe even one-note-at-a-time increments. Stopping exactly on a note or group of notes, and then adding one or two notes at a time to what you're working on, will make even some of the most ridiculous stuff possible.

Extensions and Alterations

The more time you spend with chords in the real world, the more you'll become aware that a lot of chord voicings and melody notes use more than just the 1–3–5–7 of the chord. These usually fall into the categories called "extensions" or "alterations."

If you keep stacking thirds past the 7th, you'll get the **extensions** 9, 11, and 13. You hardly ever hear all three extensions used at once in a chord, but sometimes you'll here one or two, which will make the harmony sound fuller.

Other chords, especially dominant sevenths, use notes that are not part of the regular chord symbol to create more interest and better voice leading. These are called **alterations**. The chord tones 5, 9, and 13 are usually the notes that are altered. They're raised or lowered a half step, and sometimes both.

Manufacturing Drill #21: Extensions

These eight chords start out with a normal seventh chord, then an extension is added to the same voicing for the second chord. Sing the added extension before the second voicing is played. The extension you sing can be in a different octave if necessary. Since 9, 11, and 13 are the same pitches as 2, 4, and 6, it's O.K. to think of these lower notes in order to produce the extensions.

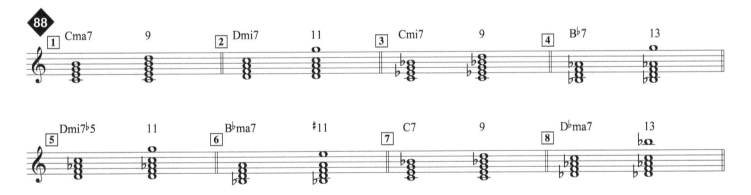

Manufacturing Drill #22: Alterations

These eight are also in pairs. We'll perform all the alterations on the same E7 chord. You'll hear the 1–3–7 voicing first. Sing the alteration that's indicated before the answer is played. Again, the octave you sing in is not as important as coming up with the right pitch. For instance, a #9 alteration sounds the same as a minor 3rd. If you have to imagine the minor 3rd to get the pitch, that's fine.

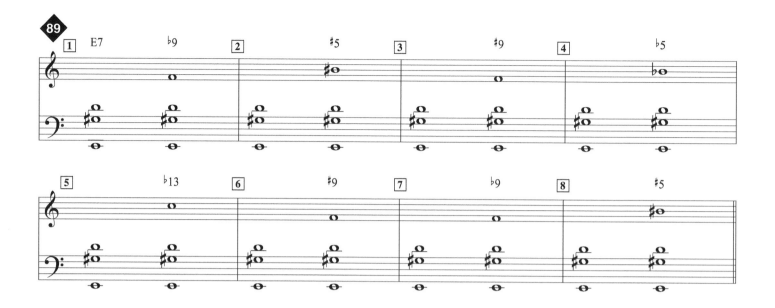

Music Transcription #4: Chords with Extensions

Here are eight chords played simultaneously, all with the same root. They're all some kind of seventh chord with an extension. Write the chord symbol with the extension.

◆90 1._____ 2._____ 3._____ 4._____

5._____ 6._____ 7._____ 8._____

Music Transcription #5: Chords with Alterations

Here are eight more chords played simultaneously, all based on the same root. These are all dominant chords with an added alteration. Write the alteration.

◆91 1._____ 2._____ 3._____ 4._____

5._____ 6._____ 7._____ 8._____

Music Transcription #6: More Extensions and Alterations

The next four progressions are each four measures long. There's one chord per measure with either an extension or alteration. Write the correct chord symbol for each measure. The starting root is given.

◆92 A ___ ___ ___ ___   ◆93 G ___ ___ ___ ___

◆94 F ___ ___ ___ ___   ◆95 D ___ ___ ___ ___

Getting Closer to Reality

Music Transcription #7: Reality Cometh

These two transcription exercises involve three parts: melody, chords, and bass. Transcribe the parts and the exact chord voicings as well—you'll probably want to start with the melody or bass first, then the chords. You might need to use some spare manuscript paper at first, and remember to try to sing and visualize the parts before you start hunting around on your instrument.

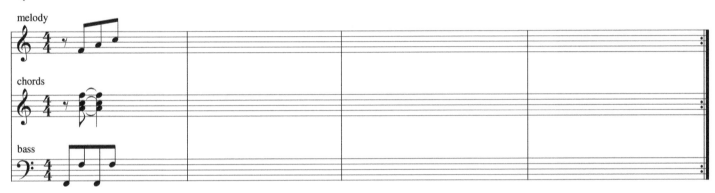

This next one has "pickup" notes that precede the first measure. These notes recur in the fourth measure of the phrase, so you can use that measure to begin transcribing.

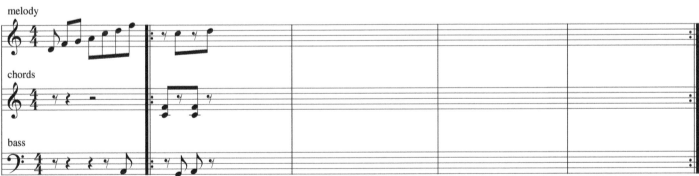

Music Transcription #8: Reality Cometh, Really

Here are a couple more transcription exercises, this time with four parts: chords, melody, bass, and guitar. Take your time. Sing and visualize.

The Real Thing

That's it. You're on your own now. Just remember, you're exposed to ear training opportunities every day: television, radio, movies, your CD collection, elevators, the Internet, telephone hold music, even the stuff floating around in your own head. If you actively listen to and visualize the music you're exposed to all the time, you can always improve and maintain that almighty connection between your ears, your imagination, and your instrument.

Good luck!

Appendix: Answer Key

7 Bass

1. P4
2. ma2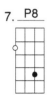
3. P5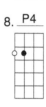
4. ma7
5. ma3
6. ma2

7. P8
8. P4
9. ma3
10. ma6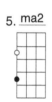
11. ma2
12. P5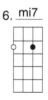

Guitar

1. P4
2. ma2
3. P5
4. ma7
5. ma3
6. ma2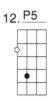

7. P8
8. P4
9. ma3
10. ma6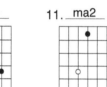
11. ma2
12. P5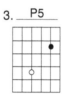

8 Bass

1. mi3
2. P4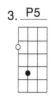
3. mi6
4. P5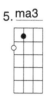
5. ma2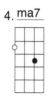
6. mi7

7. P4
8. mi3
9. P5
10. mi6
11. mi3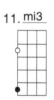
12. P8

Guitar

1. mi3
2. P4
3. mi6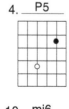
4. P5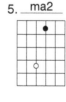
5. ma2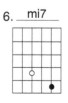
6. mi7

7. P4
8. mi3
9. P5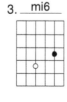
10. mi6
11. mi3
12. P8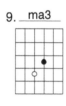

Bass

1. mi3
2. P5
3. ma7
4. P4
5. mi7
6. ma2

7. mi6
8. dim5
9. mi2
10. ma3
11. ma6
12. P5

Guitar

1. mi3
2. P5
3. ma7
4. P4
5. mi7
6. ma2

7. mi6
8. dim5
9. mi2
10. ma3
11. ma6
12. P5

Bass

1. ma6
2. P4
3. ma6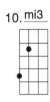
4. mi6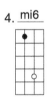
5. P5
6. aug4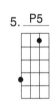

7. ma2
8. P5
9. mi7
10. mi3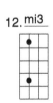
11. ma6
12. mi3

Guitar

1. ma6
2. P4
3. ma6
4. mi6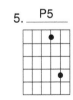
5. P5
6. aug4

7. ma2
8. P5
9. mi7
10. mi3
11. ma6
12. mi3

18

1. P4 2. ma3 3. ma6 4. mi2 5. mi3 6. ma7

7. P5 8. *TT 9. mi6 10. mi3 11. mi3 12. P4

13. P5 14. mi6 15. mi3 16. ma6 17. P4 18. mi2

19. mi7 20. TT 21. ma6 22. P5 23. ma2 24. P4

25. ma2 26. P4 27. ma7 28. mi2 29. P4 30. P4

*TT = tritone throughout (aug 4 or dim5)

 25

Bass

1. P5 2. P4 3. ma2 4. ma3 5. P4 6. mi6 7. P5 8. P4

Guitar

1. P5 2. P4 3. ma2 4. ma3 5. P4 6. mi6 7. P5 8. P4

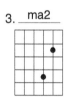

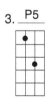 **26**

Bass

1. ma3 2. P5 3. P4 4. ma6 5. P4 6. mi2 7. P4 8. ma3

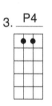

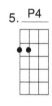
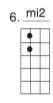
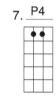

Guitar

1. ma3 2. P5 3. P4 4. ma6 5. P4 6. mi2 7. P4 8. ma3

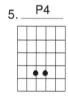

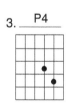

 27

Bass

1. P4 2. mi6 3. P5 4. mi3 5. P5 6. ma7 7. TT 8. P5

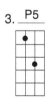
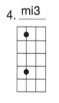
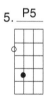
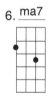

Guitar

1. P4 2. mi6 3. P5 4. mi3 5. P5 6. ma7 7. TT 8. P5

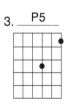
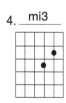

28

Bass

1. ma6   2. P4   3. ma2   4. mi3   5. ma6   6. ma3   7. P4   8. mi3

Guitar

1. ma6   2. P4   3. ma2   4. mi3   5. ma6   6. ma3   7. P4   8. mi3

       (image)

29

Bass

1. ma2   2. ma6   3. ma2   4. mi3   5. mi6   6. mi2   7. TT   8. ma2

       (image)

Guitar

1. ma2   2. ma6   3. ma2   4. mi3   5. mi6   6. mi2   7. TT   8. ma2

30 **Bass**

1. mi3   2. ma2   3. mi6   4. TT   5. ma3   6. P4

7. mi6   8. P5   9. P4   10. ma2   11. ma6   12. mi3

Guitar

1. mi3   2. ma2   3. mi6   4. TT   5. ma3   6. P4

7. mi6   8. P5   9. P4   10. ma2   11. ma6   12. mi3

  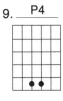

Bass

1. P4
2. mi6
3. P4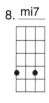
4. ma3
5. ma2
6. TT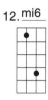

7. ma3
8. mi7
9. mi2
10. ma6
11. P4

Guitar

1. P4
2. mi6
3. P4
4. ma3
5. ma2
6. TT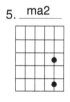

7. ma3
8. mi7
9. mi2
10. ma6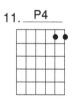
11. P4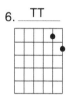
12. mi6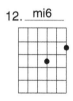

1. ma
2. mi
3. ma
4. dim
5. mi
6. ma

7. dim
8. aug
9. mi
10. ma
11. mi
12. mi

Bass

1. ma
2. mi
3. mi
4. ma
5. aug
6. dim

7. mi
8. aug
9. ma
10. dim
11. aug
12. dim

Guitar

1. ma
2. mi
3. mi
4. ma
5. aug
6. dim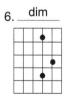

7. mi
8. aug
9. ma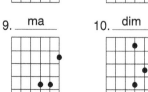
10. dim
11. aug
12. dim

Bass

1. ma
2. ma 1st
3. dim
4. mi 1st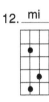
5. mi
6. dim 1st

7. ma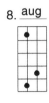
8. aug
9. ma 1st
10. mi 1st
11. dim
12. mi

Guitar

1. ma
2. ma 1st
3. dim
4. mi 1st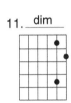
5. mi
6. dim 1st

7. ma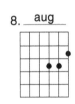
8. aug
9. ma 1st
10. mi 1st
11. dim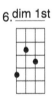
12. mi

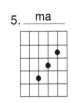 **Bass**

1. ma 1st
2. mi
3. mi 1st
4. dim
5. ma
6. dim 1st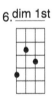

7. aug 1st
8. ma 1st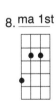
9. ma
10. dim 1st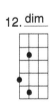
11. mi 1st
12. dim

Guitar

1. ma 1st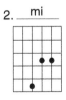
2. mi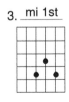
3. mi 1st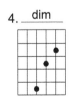
4. dim
5. ma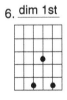
6. dim 1st

7. aug 1st
8. ma 1st
9. ma
10. dim 1st
11. mi 1st
12. dim

43 Bass

1. ma 2nd   2. ma 1st   3. ma   4. dim 1st   5. mi 2nd

   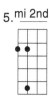

6. dim   7. aug   8. dim 2nd   9. mi   10. mi 1st

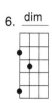   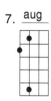

Guitar

1. ma 2nd   2. ma 1st   3. ma   4. dim 1st   5. mi 2nd

   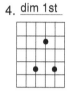

6. dim   7. aug   8. dim 2nd   9. mi   10. mi 1st

   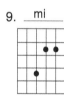

 44 Bass

1. ma 2nd   2. ma   3. mi   4. mi   5. dim   6. ma 1st

  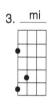 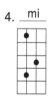 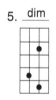 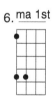

7. dim   8. aug   9. mi 2nd   10. ma 1st   11. ma 2nd   12. ma

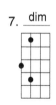 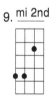 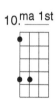 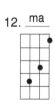

Guitar

1. ma 2nd   2. ma   3. mi   4. mi   5. dim   6. ma 1st

 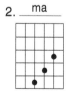 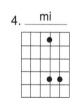 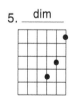 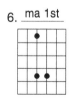

7. dim   8. aug   9. mi 2nd   10. ma 1st   11. ma 2nd   12. ma

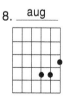    

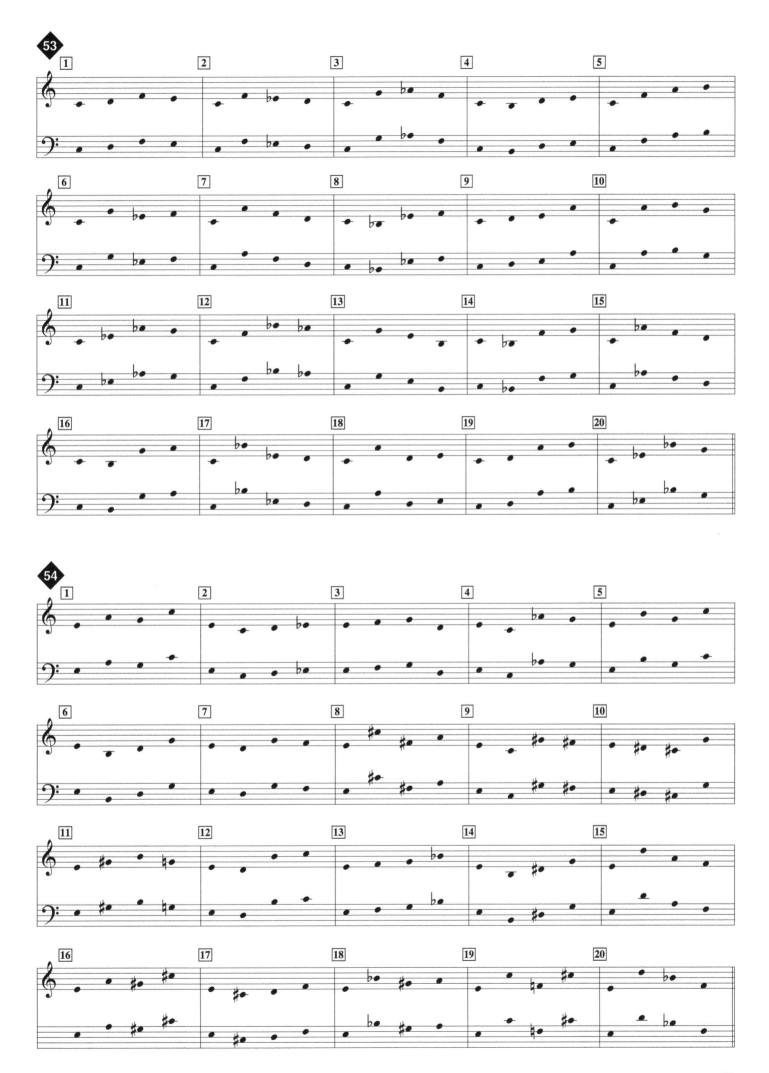

Bass

1. ___7___   2. mi7♭5   3. ma7 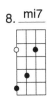 4. mi7 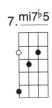 5. ___7___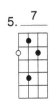

6. ma7 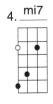 7. mi7♭5 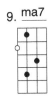 8. mi7   9. ma7 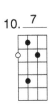 10. ___7___

Guitar

1. ___7___   2. mi7♭5   3. ma7   4. mi7   5. ___7___

6. ma7 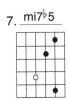 7. mi7♭5   8. mi7 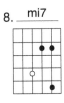 9. ma7 10. ___7___

 Bass

1. mi7 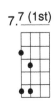 2. 7 (2nd) 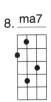 3. ma7 (3rd)   4. ___7___ 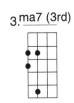 5. mi7 (3rd) 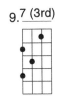 6. mi7 (2nd)

7. 7 (1st)   8. ma7   9. 7 (3rd) 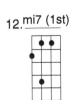 10. ma7 (2nd) 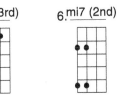 11. mi7♭5 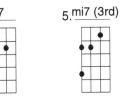 12. mi7 (1st)

Guitar

1. mi7   2. 7 (2nd)   3. ma7 (3rd) 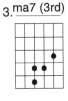 4. ___7___  5. mi7 (3rd) 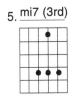 6. mi7 (2nd)

7. 7 (1st)   8. ma7   9. 7 (3rd) 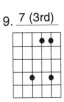 10. ma7 (2nd) 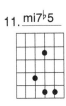 11. mi7♭5 12. mi7 (1st)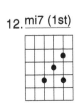

Bass

1. 7 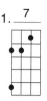 2. mi7   3. 7 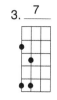 4. mi7  5. ma7  6. ma7 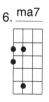 7. mi7

8. mi7♭5 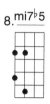 9. 7 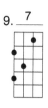 10. ma7  11. ma7 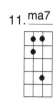 12. 7 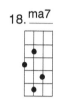 13. mi7 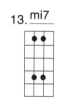 14. 7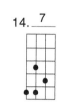

15. mi7 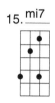 16. mi7 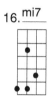 17. mi7♭5 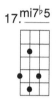 18. ma7   19. mi7♭5   20. 7

Guitar

1. 7   2. mi7 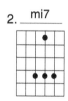 3. 7 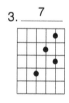 4. mi7 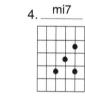 5. ma7 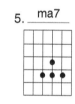 6. ma7 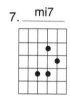 7. mi7

8. mi7♭5 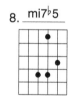 9. 7 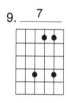 10. ma7  11. ma7 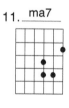 12. 7 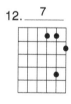 13. mi7 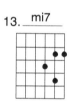 14. 7

15. mi7 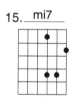 16. mi7  17. mi7♭5  18. ma7  19. mi7♭5   20. 7

  76 Dmi7 ___ G7 ___ Cma7 ___ Fma7 ___ C
key center

77 Cmi7 ___ Dmi7 ___ Gmi7 ___ E♭ma7 ___ B♭
key center

78 B♭ma7 ___ Ami7 ___ Gmi7 ___ Dmi7 ___ F
key center

  79 Gma7 ___ A7 ___ Bmi7 ___ Emi7 ___ D
key center

 80 Ami7 ___ Dmi7 ___ Emi7 ___ Ami7 ___ C
key center

81 Cma7   D7/C   G7/B   Ami7

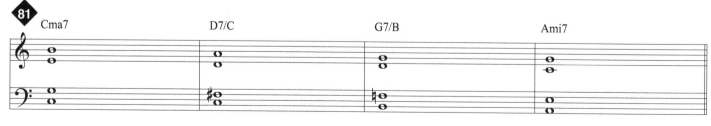

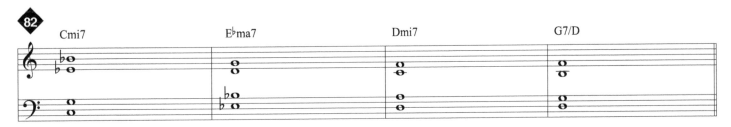

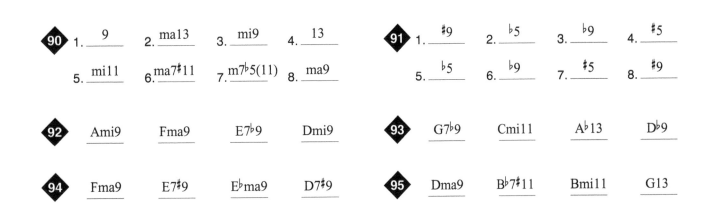